Oil

Neil Potter

Macdonald Educational

Contents

How to use this book
This book tells you about oil. In it you will find out what oil is, where it is found, how it can be used and what effects it has on the way we live. For instance, if you want to find out about refineries, you will see that refineries are on page 32. The index will tell you where and how many times a particular subject is mentioned, and whether there is a picture of it. You will find pipelines, for example, on page 28. The glossary explains the more difficult terms found in this book.

TIME SCALE	Millions of years
	Quaternary
	1
reptile	Tertiary
	70
fish	Cretaceous
	100
ammonite	Jurassic
	200
goniatite	Triassic
	Permian
	300
graptolite	Carboniferous
trilobite	Devonian
	400

The beginnings of oil

Oil, or petroleum, is a substance which is vital to our lives. It is used as a source of energy for cars, ships, motorbikes, aircraft and trains. It lubricates machinery. It is used as a heating fuel for buildings. It is needed in the manufacture of hundreds of everyday products including plastics, detergents, cosmetics, paints, medicines, pesticides and fertilizers. Without oil, life in an industrial country today would be scarcely possible.

How oil is formed

Oil is found deep in the earth or beneath the seabed. Millions of years ago, much of the land was covered by oceans. Tiny sea animals and plants died and sank to the bottom. Their remains became covered with thick layers of mud and sand which turned into rock. The pres-

◀ Over many millions of years dead animals and plants were buried in mud which hardened into rock. Crude oil was formed in these rocks.

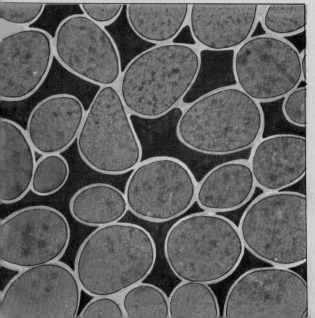

◀ Oil (black) is trapped between grains of sand (brown) in porous rocks. Water is also trapped in the pores.

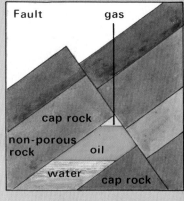

Fault   gas

cap rock

non-porous rock   oil

water   cap rock

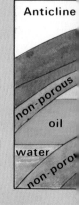

Anticline

non-porous

oil

water

non-poro

sure of this weight at very high temperatures turned these remains into tiny drops of oil and chemicals rich in carbon and hydrogen.

When the oil was being formed, it squeezed into *porous* and *permeable* rock like limestones or sandstones. Continued pressure and movements of the earth's crust forced the oil upwards and outwards until it came against impermeable rock called *cap rock* which it could not penetrate. The oil became trapped with water and gas in porous layers of rock between non-porous rock layers. Rocks which trap oil in this way are called reservoir rocks.

It is important to realize that oil is not found in vast underground lakes. It is trapped in the tiny spaces between grains of sand in porous rock in small droplets, rather as water is held in a fine sponge.

Seepages and traps

In some parts of the world, changes in the earth's crust forced oil to the surface where it lay on the surface of the water in lakes or pits. Sun and air caused the lighter parts of it to evaporate, leaving behind a deposit of thick heavy oil called bitumen. These natural oil lakes are called seepages.

Most oil and natural gas, however, stay under the earth, blocked against the reservoir rocks by traps which prevent it from escaping. Traps are formed by faults and folds in the structure of the layers of rock. The most common trap is an *anticline*. Layers of rock are folded into a dome shape through which the gas and oil cannot move.

Another form is the *fault* trap. This is caused by a vertical crack in the layers of rock which makes one side slip down. Impermeable rock is then pushed hard against the porous rock which holds the oil, forming a barrier.

In some areas, salt beds were created when ancient seas dried up. As the salt was lighter than the rocks around it, movement in the earth gradually pushed it upwards in the form of a dome. The oil and gas were trapped in the porous rock at each side. This type of trap is called a *salt dome*.

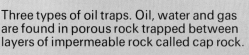
Three types of oil traps. Oil, water and gas are found in porous rock trapped between layers of impermeable rock called cap rock.

gas

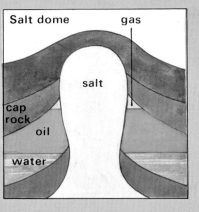
Salt dome   gas

salt

cap rock

oil

water

Bitumen on roads is one of many essential uses of oil. ▼

Oil in history

Although the oil industry is comparatively recent, oil was first discovered hundreds of years before the birth of Christ. Noah is said to have coated the Ark with layers of bitumen to make it watertight. The Babylonians used bitumen from seepages as a building material when they built the walls of Babylon in about 600 BC. The Chinese drilled for oil at the time of Julius Caesar and carried it through bamboo pipes to their cities where it was burned in lamps. The Indians in Brazil tipped their arrows with bitumen. They then set fire to them and used the burning arrows as weapons against enemy tribes or against the invading Portuguese. Bitumen was even used by Mexican Indians as a cure for stomach pains and in 1539, a barrel of oil was shipped from Venezuela to the Emperor Charles V in Europe. He suffered from gout, a painful swelling of the foot and thought that the oil might relieve his symptoms.

▲ Babylonians used bitumen as an ointment to heal wounds. Bitumen was also used in a more traditional way to pave the streets.

The *Vasa*, a 17th century ship, was found intact at the bottom of Stockholm harbour in 1956. Oil-based chemicals were used to preserve and restore the ship. ▼

In 1851 Price's candle-making works developed a distillation process which produced high quality candle from cheap raw materials. ▼

Oil for lighting

One of the most important early uses of oil was for lighting. Oil was produced in Scotland in the mid-19th century from shale and used for making candles. With the development of oil-burning lamps, however, there was a world-wide need for more oil. Whale oil was used at first but this was difficult to obtain and there was not enough to satisfy demand.

It was initially the need for paraffin for oil lamps which started the enormous oil industry in the USA in the 19th century. Paraffin was produced by distillation or boiling in simple refineries. The process of distillation also produced heavier oils which could be used for lubricating machinery and carriage axles.

One of the lighter by-products or results of distillation was petrol. At first, it was simply poured away into open pits and burned there as no-one knew of any use for it. It was only in 1885 that a petrol engine was first used to drive a car. Meanwhile, other oil by-products such as fuel oil were still being burned off. By the end of the 19th century, fuel oil was being used in factories and in the production of electricity. Oil was becoming a very important source of heat, light and power.

The pioneers

In August 1859, an American called Colonel Edwin Drake drilled a well 23 metres deep on a stream in Pennsylvania. The stream was called 'Oil Creek' because seepages of oil had been seen on the surface of the water. Drake found that his well could produce at first ten and then 25 *barrels* of oil a day (a barrel holds 160 litres of oil). The discovery of Drake's well is said to mark the true beginning of the world oil industry. Thousands of people came to look for oil, encouraged by Drake's success and a boom in oil drilling resulted. The USA became the world's first great oil-producing country.

▲ Many oil wells were drilled in Oil Creek Valley, Pennsylvania in 1865 at the beginning of the 'oil rush'.

Early drilling methods

The first oil workers used very primitive equipment. They drilled through the ground with a bell-shaped weight attached to a rope which was fastened to a pulley at the top of a tripod. At the other end of the rope, a mule raised the weight to the top. An automatic release sent the weight plunging to the ground, rather like a punch. The mule then had to pull the weight up again and the process was repeated. This method of drilling was long and slow. An additional disadvantage was that the first flow of oil when the rock split could not yet be controlled. It sometimes burst from the pressure of the underground gas and then gushed into the air and was wasted. There was also a great danger of fire. Gradually, however, drilling equipment improved and new drills were developed which could dig far deeper into the earth.

Rotary drilling

In January 1901, oil was found at a depth of 340 metres at a new well called Spindletop, at Beaumont in Texas. It flowed at the then colossal rate of 100,000 barrels a day. Within three months, the town's population of 9,000 had increased to 50,000 as eager speculators and new oil companies flocked to the town.

The Spindletop well was drilled using a new method called rotary drilling. The *bit* was no longer used as a punch but was, instead, made to revolve at the end of a long drill pipe. This bored a hole in the rock in much the same way that a modern power drill bores holes in concrete.

Oil under the sea

Drilling for oil below the seabed did not start until the 1930s when drilling platforms or rigs were built in the off-

▲ In Romania, oil wells were dug to shallow depths by hand. The diggers got fresh air from the bellows and oil was brought back up by a system of pulleys drawn by horses.

Edwin Drake in front of his well at Titusville, Pennsylvania in 1861. ▶

shore swamps of Louisiana. The first drilling platforms that were out of sight of land were in the Gulf of Mexico. Today, more than 8.5 million barrels of crude oil a day are produced from under the sea. Some geologists think that there are 200,000 million barrels still to be discovered.

Oil in Britain

The first search for oil on land in Britain began during the First World War. In 1939, a series of oil fields were found in Nottinghamshire. They are still producing today. More discoveries were later made in Dorset.

Where oil is found

After the historic discovery of Edwin Drake's well in 1859, there was an 'oil rush' similar to the gold rush that had taken place a few years earlier in California. Before long, oil was found in California, Oklahoma, Louisiana and Texas. In the first hundred years of the American oil industry, more than 1,500,000 wells were drilled. For a long time, the USA was the world's largest oil producer and half of the world's supply came from American wells. Today however, the USA uses so much oil that it has to import oil from other countries, especially Saudi Arabia.

Oil in the Soviet Union

Oil was found in Russia as early as the 18th century. The Russian industry expanded after more oil discoveries until, in 1900, the country was producing more oil than the USA. The Soviet Union is now the world's largest oil producer, at the rate of 11 million barrels a day.

▲ Exploratory drilling in South-West Iran. Oil was first found in Iran in 1908.

New discoveries of oil are being made in Canada. An artificial island is being built in the McKenzie Delta to support drilling operations. ▼

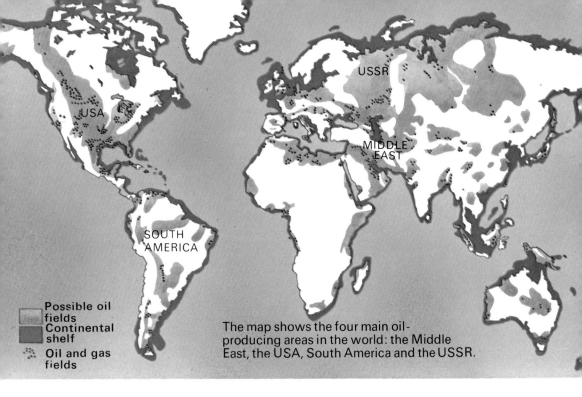

Possible oil fields
Continental shelf
Oil and gas fields

The map shows the four main oil-producing areas in the world: the Middle East, the USA, South America and the USSR.

World's oil fields

A large number of countries produce oil. It is found in several South American countries, including Venezuela, Brazil and Mexico and also in parts of the Caribbean. Oil has been found in Indonesia and also in countries in North and West Africa. Small amounts of oil are still found in Europe. Most of the oil we use, however, comes from the Middle East. This is a region which is important not only because of the oil it produces now but also because it has vast oil reserves for the future. In 1908, a company which later became British Petroleum found oil in the deserts of Iran and in 1927, oil was found in Iraq. A few years later, oil was found in Bahrain, Kuwait and in Saudi Arabia. This country now produces nine million barrels a day and has a quarter of the world's known oil reserves. There are still 150,000 million barrels to be produced.

North Sea oil and gas

In 1959, a big gas field was found in the Netherlands and a search for oil began. Gas fields were discovered off the coast of Norfolk but the biggest and most recent oil and gas finds have been in the North Sea, off the coast of Scotland. There are now 12 oil fields in British waters producing over a million barrels of oil a day. Within a very short time, the yield should be enough to supply all the oil needed in Britain and much of its gas.

Supply and demand

Once oil has been taken from the ground, it cannot be replaced. The demand for oil is gradually becoming greater than the supply and some experts think the world's oil supplies will run out by the year 2000. Meanwhile, the search for oil continues. New discoveries have been made in Alaska, Canada, China and off the coast of Australia.

The work of the geologist

The prospectors and speculators who searched for oil in the 19th century worked mainly by instinct, guess-work or past experience. They had neither detailed knowledge of rock structures nor scientific instruments and they lacked equipment for digging deep into the earth. They tended to work in areas where there were already ancient seepages of oil. This limited exploration. Today, however, prospecting for oil is a highly skilled and scientific operation and all sorts of modern instruments and methods are used. As a result, a large number of new oil fields have been discovered.

Geological investigations

The search for oil starts with the work of the geologist, a person who studies the earth's crust and its history. He builds up a geological map of an area where oil may be trapped within rock formations. This area may be the desert, the Arctic, swampy forests, jungle or mountains. Aerial photographs are then taken from an aircraft flying to and fro over the land surface to find out more about its shape. These photographs are worked into

◀ Geologists taking a land survey in Alaska.

▲ A geologist is studying samples of rocks.

another map which gives further clues about the structure and type of the rocks underneath. The geologist will then need to visit the region himself. Armed with his geologist's hammer to chip off pieces of rock as well as his hand-lens and other instruments, he has to climb mountains and cliffs and explore rivers and deserts. This can be a very lonely job and the geologist may have to spend years in remote and isolated areas. Working conditions can be extremely difficult. Daytime temperatures in the desert can reach 55°C so that tools become too hot to handle and the geologist also has to face scorching desert winds and sandstorms.

After the heat of the desert, the geologist may be transferred to the Arctic where he has to work in frozen wastes in temperatures of −50°C. The cold can make it difficult to breathe and metal instruments may break like twigs. All these investigations are the vital first stage in the search for oil.

The geophysicist

The geophysicist carries out the second stage in the search for oil. He has to build up a picture of the rock formations beneath the surface of the earth. Each type of rock has different characteristics. The geophysicist follows up the work of the geologist with specialized techniques and instruments. A magnetometer measures changes in the magnetic field caused by the presence of magnetic materials. It can also show that certain materials such as iron ore deposits may be present. A gravimeter, which is an instrument rather like a sensitive spring balance, gives the geophysicist additional information about the nature and shape of rocks. Heavier, denser rocks cause greater pull downwards than lighter rocks and the gravimeter shows how the pull of gravity varies from place to place.

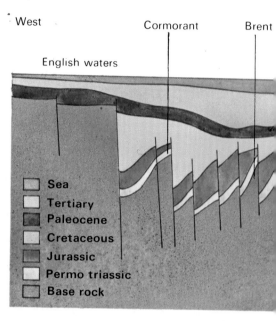

West

English waters

Cormorant

Brent

Sea
Tertiary
Paleocene
Cretaceous
Jurassic
Permo triassic
Base rock

▲ Geological cross-section of the North sea oil basin at 61° latitude, 80 km east of Northern Shetland, and 58° 30′ latitude, 112 km east of Wick. The section shows the faults in the rocks. They contain a lot of oil but it is difficult to judge where to drill for it. The vertical lines in the diagram show where wells have been drilled.

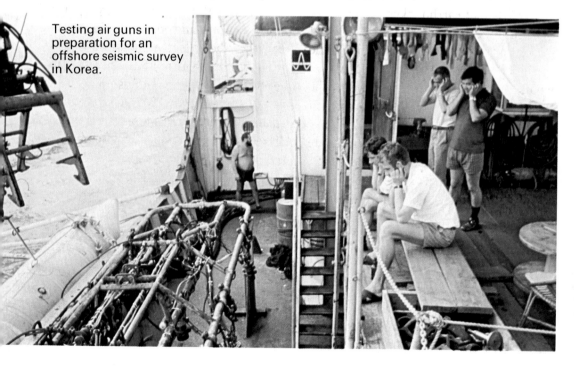

Testing air guns in preparation for an offshore seismic survey in Korea.

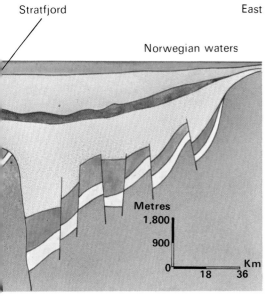

Stratfjord

East

Norwegian waters

Metres
1,800
900
0
18   36
Km

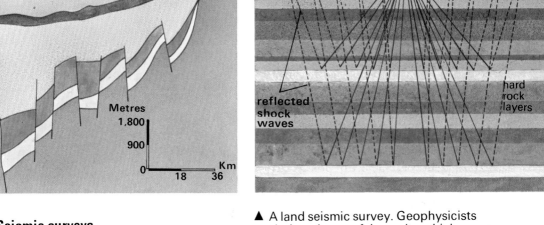

recording truck

explosion

shot firer

geophones

reflected
shock
waves

hard
rock
layers

▲ A land seismic survey. Geophysicists explode a charge of dynamite which causes waves to bounce back to the surface from the layers of rocks below. By measuring the time the waves take to come back, they can tell whether the rocks are flat or sloping for instance.

Seismic surveys

The most important method of investigation used by the geophysicist is the *seismic survey*. A seismograph is a small pendulum which moves when the ground vibrates. It is also used to measure the force of distant earthquakes. A charge of dynamite is put into a hole drilled between 10 and 100 metres into the earth. The explosion creates shock waves which travel downwards through the rock layers. Each wave bounces back an echo which is picked up by a series of sensitive recording instruments inside the seismographs, called geophones. These are laid out in a straight line on either side of the hole. They show the shock waves as jagged lines on a magnetic tape. The geophysicist can then get a clearer idea of the nature of the rock layers at different depths. This sort of investigation is called seismic reflection prospecting.

At sea, similar methods are used. Shock waves from explosions just below the surface of the water travel downwards to the seabed and through the rocks beneath. The reflected shock waves are picked up by hydrophones (similar to geophones) towed behind a ship.

Processing the information

All seismic recordings have to be processed by computer before they can be studied by the geologist and the geophysicist. Sometimes as much as 3,500 km of seismic tracings may have been 'shot' in one region. Even when it seems very likely that there is oil trapped beneath the earth or sea, no-one can be totally sure until further tests are carried out. The only way to find out for certain is to drill an exploratory hole called a *wildcat* well.

Drilling

The main feature of a drilling *rig* is the *derrick*. This is a framework of steel girders 40 metres high. It supports the drill pipe, raising and lowering it into the exploration hole. The drill pipe carries the drill bit—the toothed-steel cone which bites into the rock. At ground level, the drill pipe is clamped to a steel rotary table driven by powerful engines. The table turns the drill pipe. As the drill gradually moves downwards, more and more sections of pipe have to be added. These form the drill string. Each section is 10 metres long and the drill string may extend in sections to depths of thousands of metres.

The mud brought back to the surface contains tiny bits of rock. It is being screened to remove drill cuttings. ▼

The bit

Drill bits have three or four rollers with long or short teeth to cut into the rock. Long teeth are used for soft rocks and shorter teeth for harder formations. A special bit studded with industrial diamonds is used to bite through very hard rock. A bit usually lasts for about 30 hours although a diamond-studded bit may last for 100 hours or more. When it has to be changed and a new one put on, the whole of the drill string has to be pulled up. This can take as long as 15 hours.

During drilling, a form of *mud* is pumped down inside the drill pipe. The mud passes through jets in the drill bit into the bottom of the hole. It is then forced back to the surface outside the drill pipe. This cools the drill bit and makes sure that the pressure at the surface is the same as that at the bottom of the hole. At the same time, rock cuttings are brought back up to the surface and these are examined by a geologist. They can tell him a lot about the rock levels and the chances of finding oil down the hole. As drilling continues, the hole is lined with lengths of steel called *casing* which are cemented in place.

It can take up to a year to drill a very deep well 9 km deep and even when it is finished, no oil may be found. The chances of striking oil are about one in ten for every hole drilled.

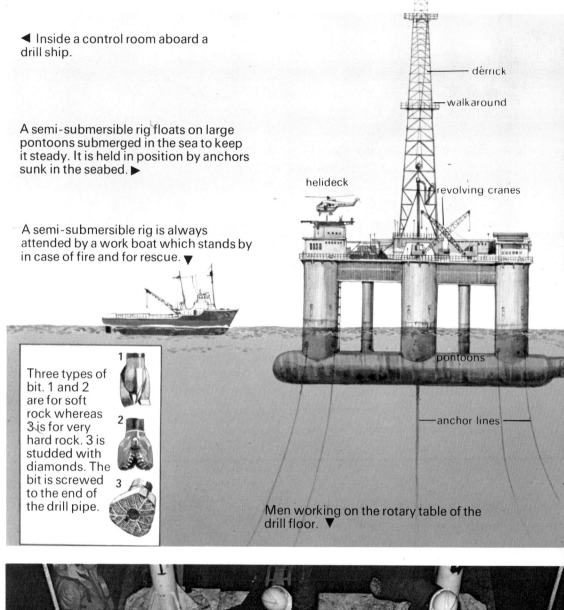

◄ Inside a control room aboard a drill ship.

A semi-submersible rig floats on large pontoons submerged in the sea to keep it steady. It is held in position by anchors sunk in the seabed. ►

A semi-submersible rig is always attended by a work boat which stands by in case of fire and for rescue. ▼

derrick

walkaround

helideck

revolving cranes

pontoons

anchor lines

Three types of bit. 1 and 2 are for soft rock whereas 3 is for very hard rock. 3 is studded with diamonds. The bit is screwed to the end of the drill pipe.

1

2

3

Men working on the rotary table of the drill floor. ▼

Oil production

Once oil has been found beneath the seabed, the company in charge has to decide how large the field is, how the oil will be moved to the shore and whether the field is worth developing in the first place. It takes six years from the first oil discovery before the field is in production and earning money for the company. Also costs are very high. No risks can be taken and the company needs to find out as much as possible about the field and the quality of the oil before any further drilling takes place. A big oil field in the North Sea costs more than £1,000 million to set up before the first barrel of oil is sold.

The production platform

Once an oil field is known to be worth developing, a production *platform* has to be built and then put in place on the field. Production platforms are like islands in the sea. They house all the equipment needed to extract the oil and pump it to the shore. This includes drilling tools, generators for electrical power, instruments to measure the flow of oil and machinery to separate the salt water, oil and gas. There will also be laboratories, a radio station and a helicopter landing deck. A *flare* stack at the top of the platform burns away gas which cannot be piped to the shore.

Most important of all, the platform controls the production wells which drain the field. There may be up to 40 wells on one platform. Platforms can be made of steel or concrete.

One of the biggest offshore production platforms ever built was towed by five tugs to its destination in the North Sea in 1975. Swirling layers of fog surround the platform.

Constructing the platforms

Steel platforms are built on land and then floated out to sea on their side. Once in the right place, they are up-ended by flooding the tanks that helped them to float. Their legs then rest firmly on the seabed, pinned down by steel piles. Equipment is lifted on by giant floating cranes.

Concrete platforms, which can weigh up to 600,000 tonnes, are built in deep water close to the shore. They are then towed by tugs to the field where their great weight holds them securely on the seabed. Concrete platforms are usually used in deeper waters. They have to be built to stay in place for 25 years, which is the average life of an oil field.

The oil flow

Once the platform is ready, the production wells are drilled and then a complicated series of valves called a *Christmas tree* is fitted. This controls the flow of oil from the wells.

The oil is pumped from the production wells through pipelines to the central platform. It is then moved to the shore, either by tanker or through a big pipeline.

Oil quantities

The amount of oil produced from a field varies a great deal, according to the size of the field. British Petroleum's 'Forties' field, which is 200 km off the coast of Scotland, produces 500,000 barrels each day. This is enough oil to fly a large aircraft sixty times across the Atlantic and back, to heat 1,000,000 houses for a day or to provide three days' fuel for the British iron and steel industry.

▲ Hoisting supplies aboard the platform.

Fireproof lifeboats carry out practice drills to ensure the safety of the crew at all times. ▼

Divers

Divers are vital in operations to get oil from under the sea. They are needed to take photographs under water, to place and repair equipment and to examine the structure of the production platform. They have to be skilled technicians, welders, mechanics and engineers and a good diver can earn £20,000 a year.

How divers work

In shallow waters, divers simply use a wet suit and breathing equipment. They live on board the platform and wait to be called to perform a particular task. In deeper waters, however, a diver needs to be protected from the strong underwater pressure as well as from the cold.

Diving bells called submersibles have been invented. These work rather like miniature submarines. They take the diver down in atmospheric conditions which are the same as those on the surface and he may live in the submersible for weeks on end. He breathes a mixture of oxygen and a gas called helium. Some submersibles have special equipment which allows them to be fixed to the legs of the production platform, instead of having to work from the seabed.

Observation submersibles

Some machines, called observation submersibles, have a large front window and large portholes to give an all-round view (see illustration on page 23). They are fitted with cameras which can take underwater pictures as well as with instruments which record information. Observation submersibles can go down to a depth of

▲ Diving bells are used to inspect the seabed around the rig and carry out repairs.

Divers inside the decompression chamber are getting back to normal pressure again. ▼

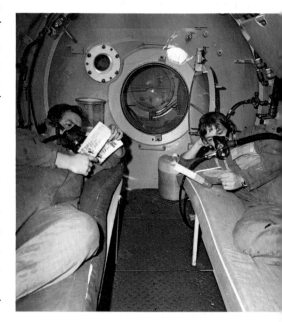

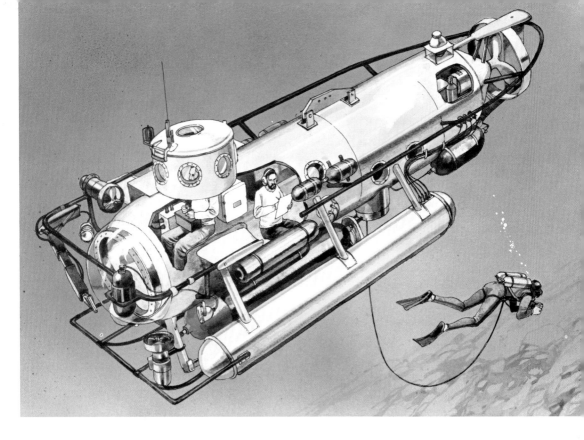

1,000 metres and are used for surveying the route of a pipeline and inspecting it for damage.

▲ Submersibles like this one are able to carry out more complicated diving jobs than the diving bell on page 22. The pilot at the front of the machine controls the activity of the divers during the dive.

Atmospheric diving suits

When conventional diving bells are used, the diver has to spend up to 14 days in a special room called a *decompression* chamber when he comes back up to the surface. This is because he has been working at pressures far greater than those at the surface and his body needs time to adjust. For every 30 metres the diver goes down, he has to spend about one day in decompression. This wastes a lot of time. New diving equipment called an atmospheric diving suit has now been developed. This suit allows a diver to go straight down and work at depths of up to 500 metres and then to surface immediately without spending time in a decompression chamber. The suit has articulated arms and hydraulically-powered 'claws' which can open and close valves. It weighs 500 kg and divers wearing these suits can also hover in the water where necessary.

Machines

Diving is, however, very dangerous. Since 1971, 33 divers have died in the North Sea alone and machines have now been invented which can go down without a diver at all. They are fitted with remote-controlled arms which can turn valves or cut cables, operated from a ship on the surface.

helicopter pilot   driller   welder   roustabout   diver   tool pusher

Life aboard a platform

A production platform may be more than 500 km from the nearest shore. It is cut off from the world except for radio and daily helicopter links. Weather conditions, especially in winter, can be extremely bad with strong winds and huge waves. Up to 200 men will live on a production platform, in very cramped conditions. This is because the platform also has to accommodate a very large amount of equipment. The men work 12 hour shifts each day for a fortnight. They are then flown ashore by helicopter for a fortnight at home. Work on a platform is dangerous, exhausting and dirty and the men are never far away from the constant noise of machinery and pumps.

The crew

Men of different skills work on the platform. The man in charge of all the drilling is the *tool pusher* who is directly responsible for the work done by the drilling

▲ Some members of the crew on a typical oil rig. Each one has his own job to do to ensure the smooth running of the rig.

ballast man

drilling superintendent

crew. The *driller* makes the hole and operates the drilling controls. The main work force is made up of men called *roughnecks*. They work on the drill floor and handle casing, pipe and other heavy plant. The *roustabouts* are the general unskilled labourers. A platform will also need engineers, radio operators, divers, electricians, mechanics, geologists, crane operators and, above all cooks. The standard of food on a platform has to be very high if the men are to work well. If food and accommodation are not found satisfactory, the work force may go and work for another company.

Recreation

When the men finish their shifts, they can watch television, see films, play billiards, darts or cards or even go fishing over the side. Much of the time, however, they will be far too tired to want to do anything but sleep. On some oil fields now, separate floating 'hotels' are built, joined to the main platform by a long walkway. This gives the men a chance to escape to a more peaceful atmosphere, away from the thud of the equipment.

Meal times aboard the rig are very popular. Special efforts are made to provide quantities of good food. ▶

Transport and communications

Most oil fields are a very long way from roads and towns. They may be in deserts or jungles and some are in mountains or in frozen Arctic regions. An offshore platform may be 500 km from the nearest coast. This means that everything needed for drilling has to be transported to the site before any work can begin. This is a lengthy and expensive process. Often, roads have to be built and whole areas of jungle cleared to provide supply routes for heavy machinery and equipment. Aircraft, ships and lorries carry everything from nuts and bolts to entire drilling rigs. It can take fleets of lorries to move a drilling rig from one site to another but new rigs have now been developed which can be lifted complete by helicopter and moved to a new location.

Helicopter services

Helicopters are used to bring supplies to places, for example jungle areas, which would otherwise be inaccessible by conventional aircraft, ship or lorry. They are also a vital part of work on a production platform. Helicopter pilots fly crew members to and from the rig and also carry stores of fresh food. They have to be on call 24 hours a day to provide an ambulance service or to

▲ These large aerials in Aberdeen are receiving micro-wave signals from the oil rig platform of the Forties field. This system of communication is called *trans-horizontal radio.*

▲ The helicopter is bringing a new crew to relieve the hard-working men on the rig.

fly in spare parts. There are about 40,000 helicopter flights a year in the North Sea alone, carrying 50,000 passengers to offshore rigs and platforms.

Supply boats

All heavy supplies such as drill bits, drill pipe and chemicals are carried to offshore platforms in supply boats. These are tough strong ships which are specially built to stand up to high winds and very rough seas. Unloading them in bad weather can be very dangerous. It may take a supply ship two days to reach a production platform from the mainland and they are therefore not used to transport urgently-needed materials.

Communications

It is essential for the crew of a platform to be able to send technical information back to base headquarters on land. In the past, this was done using radio telephones and teleprinters but these methods are not possible with platforms that are far out at sea. A new system has been developed called *trans-horizon radio* for communications between the platform and the base.

◀ Supply boats provide the rig with the necessary spare parts for drilling operations.

Pipelines

Pipelines are rather like the lifelines of the oil industry. They take the crude oil from where it is produced to where it is needed. There are about 1·5 million km of pipelines in the world. They have to be built across deserts, through mountains, under rivers and oceans, across swamps and over land. Where possible, they are buried underground so that the countryside is not spoilt.

Pipelines are made of steel and vary in diameter from 25 cm to 122 cm. They are formed from sections which are 12 metres long, joined together by welding. The welds have to be tested to make sure that there are no leaks. One way of doing this is to send a machine along inside which crawls through taking X-ray pictures of every weld.

The Trans-Alaska pipeline
One pipeline, in Alaska, runs for 1,300 km from the oil field at Prudhoe Bay to the port at Valdez. More than half of the pipeline is built above the ground on supports. This is partly to prevent the heat of the oil from thawing the permafrost, a mixture of gravel, rock and ice which lies beneath the frozen surface. The vegetation of the region depends on it. In addition, herds of 500,000 caribou (North American reindeer) move across the region each year. The pipeline has to be raised so that they can pass underneath.

The route of the pipeline had to be changed in one part as it would have passed through a sheep-breeding area. In another region, the site of a construction camp had to be changed to avoid disturbing the nesting areas of Peregrine falcons and other birds.

Building the pipeline
The Trans-Alaska pipeline is protected by a layer of glass fibre and then covered with a jacket of galvanized steel. As the

This submersible pipe-laying barge was used to lay pipelines which carry gas from the Brent oil and gas field to St. Fergus in Scotland. ▼

oil is pumped through at a speed of 11 km per hour, it is constantly watched by instruments and computers. These show if there is a leak anywhere along the line. Valves are used to prevent oil losses. If any oil were to leak, it would not only be wasteful but would also damage the vegetation and harm wildlife. At one time 18,000 people, including 1,900 women were at work building the pipeline. More than 17,000 machines, including hydraulic excavators, ditch diggers and rock cutters were used.

Pipelines under the sea

Pipelines which have to carry oil under the sea are first coated on land with paint to protect them from rust. They are then covered with concrete to help keep them down under the water. The pipe is loaded on to a barge called a *lay barge* where the sections are welded together. The completed pipeline is then buried in trenches so that it cannot be damaged by a ship's anchor or a fishing trawl. Special machines are used to dig and cover over the trenches.

▲ Construction of a pipeline on the Libyan coast.

More than 650 km of pipelines were built in Alaska. The pipelines are built above the ground on supports. Caribou can then pass underneath. ▼

Tankers

After the start of the oil boom in the USA in 1859, simple refineries were built to produce paraffin for lamps. This was needed all over the world and had to be transported by sea. At first, the paraffin was carried in barrels in wooden sailing ships but the dangers of fire from such an inflammable cargo were very great. Eventually, special oil-carrying ships were developed to carry the oil in tanks. The *Glückauf*, built in 1893, was the first oil tanker and weighed 2,000 tonnes. Today, tankers can be 400 metres long and can carry two million barrels of oil on each voyage. A tanker's main cargo space is divided up into small compartments. This is to prevent the oil from swirling around and breaking the sides of the ship.

Why tankers are so big

Before 1945, crude oil was refined in the countries where it was produced and the refined oil products were then shipped to the countries which needed them. Since the end of the Second World War however, oil has become the most commonly-used industrial fuel and the demand for crude oil in bulk has continued to rise. Refineries are now built in the oil-consuming countries. Oil is such an important fuel that about half the ships used are oil tankers and they need to be able to carry enormous quantities of oil. One of the largest tankers in the world carries 750,000 tonnes of oil from the Persian Gulf to different refineries in Europe.

Supertankers

The largest of the tankers are too big to be able to get into most ports as they need very deep water when they are fully loaded. Their cargo is so heavy that the keel or 'backbone' of the ship may almost touch the seabed in shallower water. Some of the oil therefore has to be transferred into smaller tankers which then carry the crude oil into the port. A big supertanker with about two million barrels of oil on board will arrive in a sheltered bay and smaller tankers will come alongside. The cargo is moved at a rate of 40,000 barrels an hour from the larger to the smaller tankers. This continues until the supertanker is empty or light enough to sail into the port.

Diagram showing how the tanker is divided into separate sections to prevent the oil from swirling about. ▼

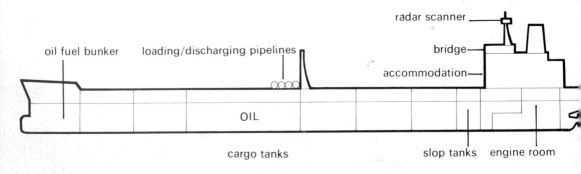

oil fuel bunker   loading/discharging pipelines   radar scanner   bridge   accommodation   OIL   cargo tanks   slop tanks   engine room

Safety precautions

Carrying oil is very dangerous and great care has to be taken to avoid fires or explosions. Even an empty tanker will still carry a great deal of highly dangerous gas vapour. A spark or charge of electricity may cause this to explode and several tankers have blown up, causing great damage and loss of life. There are now new systems of controlling the gas to prevent explosions and special equipment is used involving chemical foam to fight fires.

There is a real danger of a tanker colliding with another ship, especially in the narrow Straits of Dover between England and France. Each day, 50 tankers sail through these waters and a 'one-way' system using lanes like those on a motorway has been adopted. Coastguards and helicopter pilots act as 'policemen', reporting any ship which is in the wrong lane. Supertankers are so large that they can take up to seven kilometres to stop. Because of their size it is difficult for them to change direction.

Tankers are also used for carrying natural gas. This is liquified and kept at $-161°C$. It is carried in insulated tanks rather like giant thermos flasks. Tankers which carry natural gas are called LNG carriers.

The oil tanker 'Serenia' is loading crude oil from a buoy mooring in the Auk field, North Sea. ▶

The 'Conch' tanker was one of the earlier tankers. It was built in 1892. ▼

Refineries

The crude oil that is produced from under the ground or beneath the seabed is not much use on its own. This is because oil is a mixture of different substances which have to be separated and treated before they can be used. Crude oil has to be refined or broken up into separate parts called fractions. This happens at a refinery.

A refinery is a factory consisting of a number of tall silver-painted columns, hundreds of pipes and rows of round grey storage tanks. A typical refinery will pump over 30 million litres of crude oil into processing units each day. Two types of equipment are then used. The first separates the various products in crude oil by a physical method. The second converts one substance into another using a chemical change.

A general view of a refinery showing the large storage tanks for crude oil and the distillation units.▼

Distillation

The physical method of separating the products in crude oil is called distillation. Crude oil is first heated in a furnace to a temperature of 400°C. This turns 75 per cent of the oil into gas or vapour and the rest remains as heavy liquid. The vapour is passed through a pipe into a tall tower called a distillation column or a fractionating tower. The heaviest part of the oil, which does not turn into vapour, collects at the bottom of the column.

The distillation column is divided into 'floors' with several compartments on each floor. There are holes in the floor which allow vapour to pass through. Each of the substances in crude oil has a different boiling point and the substances can therefore be separated by heat. This is done by controlling the temperature on each floor so that the compartments get hotter towards the bottom of the column. The parts of oil with the highest boiling point condense first and the vapour is drawn off through pipes. All the way up the column, liquids of different boiling

Crude oil distillation

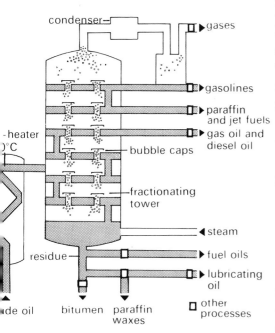

condenser — ▶ gases

▶ gasolines

▶ paraffin and jet fuels

▶ gas oil and diesel oil

-heater
)°C

bubble caps

fractionating tower

◀ steam

residue — ▶ fuel oils

▶ lubricating oil

de oil   bitumen   paraffin waxes   □ other processes

▲ In the distillation process crude oil is heated in a furnace and turned into vapour. It then passes into a column divided up into trays or 'fractions'. Oil contains many different substances. As the substances cool in the tower, they turn back into various liquids and gases. Separate products are then formed.

points are collected at different levels. Bitumen, asphalt and tar are at the lowest level, then lubricating oils, then gas oil and diesel oil, then paraffin and jet fuel, then petrol and finally, at the top, refinery gas which is burnt away in a flare.

Distillation produces more heavy oil than is needed and not enough of the lighter oils such as petrol. A chemical method called catalytic cracking is used to break up some of the heavy oils into lighter products.

How oil products are used

In the early days of oil production, refineries were quite simple and produced mainly paraffin for lamps. When cars became popular at the beginning of the 20th century, petrol was needed. With the development of industry, however, heavier oils were needed. The use of gas and later electricity for lighting meant that there was less demand for lamp oil. Instead, fuel oil was needed for industry and in the production of electricity. By the 1930s, diesel oil was needed for buses and lorries. This is known today as DERV, which stands for Diesel Engined Road Vehicles. The development of jet aircraft in the 1950s led to an increased demand for highly refined paraffin.

Where refineries are built

Most refineries today are built on the coast so that tankers carrying crude oil can reach them. If the refinery is near to an oil field, the crude oil may be brought in through a pipeline. The refined products are taken away by smaller tankers or pipelines or by road and rail.

33

Products from oil

Some of the substances which are separated when crude oil is refined can form the basis of other products. An enormous industry called the *petrochemical* industry makes substances which we all need in our daily lives. These are made from petroleum products, using physical and chemical processes.

The petrochemical industry developed during the Second World War when rubber, then urgently needed for tyres, could not be obtained from plantations in Malaya and the East Indies. Synthetic or artificial rubber was made as a substitute, using petroleum products. Nylon was developed as a substitute for cotton and silk. These new materials became widely used even when they were no longer needed as substitutes.

Everyday objects

Today, it would be hard to think of many objects in everyday use that were not made from petrochemical products. Plastics of all sorts form a large group, including containers, toys, telephones, kitchen utensils, furniture, shower curtains, swimming pools, etc. . . The ingredients in washing-up liquid, household cleaners, paints, inks and dyes, drugs and medicines, cosmetics, shampoo and fertilizer are also an important part of the petrochemical industry. In addition, most of the clothes we wear are partly or entirely made from man-made fibres such as polyester, acrylic, acetate, courtelle and nylon. All these are made from oil-based products.

Food from oil

Scientists in oil companies are constantly searching for new by-products. They have now found a way of manufacturing synthetic protein, using oil. Protein is essential for growth and is found in foods such as eggs, meat and fish. Protein based on oil is already used for making animal feeds and may well be used before long for making food for people. This will be especially important in parts of the world where people cannot obtain or afford adequate protein.

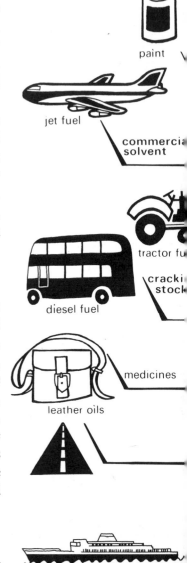

paint

jet fuel

commercia solvent

tractor fu

cracki stock

diesel fuel

medicines

leather oils

marine bunker fuel

Some of the main uses of oil. As the chart shows the number and variety of products is enormous.

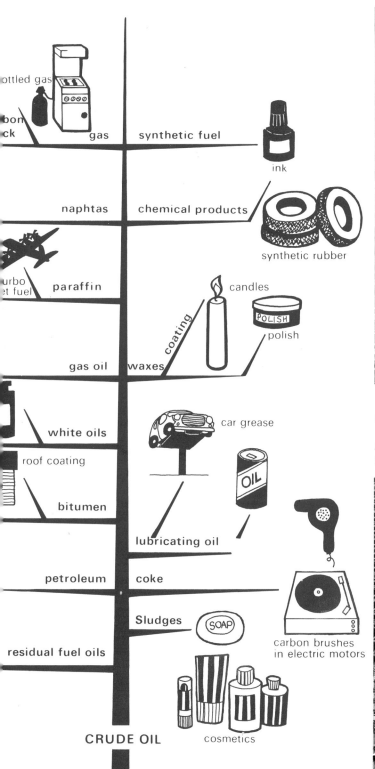

ottled gas

bon
ck

gas   synthetic fuel

ink

naphtas   chemical products

synthetic rubber

urbo
et fuel   paraffin

candles

coating

POLISH

polish

gas oil   waxes

white oils

car grease

roof coating

OIL

bitumen

lubricating oil

petroleum   coke

Sludges   SOAP

carbon brushes
in electric motors

residual fuel oils

CRUDE OIL   cosmetics

▲ Wax is one of many
oil-based products.

A toy oil rig made of
plastic. ▼

Pollution

In 1967, a big tanker called the *Torrey Canyon* ran against rocks near the Scilly Isles, off the southwest coast of Britain. The rocks tore a great hole in the side of the tanker and 95,000 tonnes of oil spilled out into the sea. The oil was carried by the winds and tide until it reached the beaches of Devon and Cornwall. It then spread across the English Channel to the Brittany coast in France. Thousands of sea birds and fish died as they became soaked in the thick oil. Holiday beaches were covered with a foul-smelling sticky black tide.

This accident and its consequences took the marine authorities completely by surprise. They had no methods or organization for dealing with such a catastrophe. Since then, there have been several other accidents where tankers have either run aground or have collided with other ships. In 1978 the Amoco Cadiz tanker ran aground near Brittany. All the oil cargo had to be released before the clean up could begin.

Why accidents happen

There are seven thousand tankers sailing the seas, many of which carry over half a million tonnes of oil. They frequently have to sail through very narrow stretches of water that are crowded with ships. Over 300,000 ships, for example, pass through the English Channel each year. Tankers are normally staffed by a crew of only 30. Safety precautions are not always observed and this adds greatly to the risk of a collision.

Non-accidental pollution

It is not only accidents to tankers which cause pollution on a vast scale. Some tanker crews disregard regulations about where waste products may be emptied. When a tanker is empty, oil still clings to the sides of the compartments and has to be washed off. The mixture of oil and water that is left after cleaning should be kept on board and unloaded only at the next tanker terminal when the tanker takes on a new cargo. Some crews however, discharge the waste straight into the sea.

The *Amoco Cadiz* tanker ran aground in 1978, spilling 230,000 tonnes of oil into the Channel. This reached many of the Brittany beaches, destroying wild life and seriously affecting the tourist industry. ▶

These gannets covered in oil have just been rescued from the Island of Grassholm. They have been wrapped up in plastic bags to prevent them from preening the deadly oil from their feathers. They have rubber bands round their beaks too. ▼